TWO

One Destined to
Addiction the Other to be Free

Alexander T. Polgar Ph.D.

SANDRIAM
PUBLICATIONS

Sandriam Publications Inc.
Hamilton, Ontario, Canada

TWO: One Destined to Addiction the Other to be Free by
Alexander T. Polgar Ph.D.

© 2019 Sandriam Publications Inc.
183 St. Clair Blvd.
Hamilton, Ontario Canada
L8M 2N9

sandriampublications.com

ISBN: 978-0-9730389-3-4

Printed and bound in Canada
Cover: Workhorse Design Studio

ALSO BY
ALEXANDER T. POLGAR PH.D.

Conducting Parenting Capacity Assessments: A Manual for Mental Health Professionals

Chronobiology: Strategies for Coping with Shift Work

Because We Can – We Must: Achieving the Human Developmental Potential in Five Generations

This work is dedicated to all those who struggle with being an addicted addict trying to first understand and then do something about their condition

CONTENTS

WE ARE SALLY AND ROBERT

I am Sally the addict. On most days I look like the girl next door. There is nothing about me that screams out "look out for that girl, she is trouble". As a result people expect of me to behave in ways I can do for a little while but never for long. Being an addict always got in the way until I finally accepted my reality. My reality is that the absence that defines me is life enduring but I am not alone. The fellowship that comes from not being alone will be crucially important later but that is a story for another time. For now, all you need to know is that once I accepted who I am and decided to do what is necessary for someone like me to turn my life around everything became tremendously better. So, there is good reason for hope and for never forgetting it.

I am Robert, the non-addict in our life stories. I look like most guys my age although sometimes scruffy according to my mom. I play as many sports I can fit into my schedule. My school marks are pretty good and I hardly get into trouble. Mostly I get into trouble at home for being a slob. All in all I consider myself to be extremely lucky to had been born into my family. I realize that by random chance I got parents who were and continue to be capable of providing me with the right kind of love and experiences necessary for developing the potential with which I was born. What I got as a child will serve me well throughout my life.

Our story is about how all parents, including us when we became parents, repeat the mistakes or the successes of their own family's past history not because of some physical condition like genes, but because of what they learned. How each one of us turns out therefore, is simply the luck of the draw as to which family we are born into.

Yes we know there is no perfect family and that all parents, to various degrees, fail to protect the perfection with which we're born to them. The key term is; *to various degrees*. Each of our stories represent the extreme not merely for impact but to show that extreme negative experiences are the norm not the exception. Sadly, the extreme positive experiences are the exceptions. Our aim is to reverse that.

We want this to be as powerful a message as possible. So we will focus on one crucially important outcome to the different environments to which we were each exposed. We do not want to play down the other later-life negative consequences to early life experiences. For certain there are many. What we want to show most of all is how one of us was systematically programmed to be an addict. The other was programmed to be resilient and confident about being able to rise to life's challenges.

While we want you to care about us as people what we really want you to care about is our story and the message in it. The message being; "there but for my good luck to be born into this family I could have been born into another family and made to be an addict who becomes addicted". We believe ours is a good message because it is a message of hope and power. Since luck is random there is nothing we can do about that. But we can certainly do something about the environments we create for our children and how well we parent them to become the adults for which they have the potential. We also believe, and Sally is the proof, that even made addicts can become and stay sober if they do what is required of them.

Our purpose for starting our story with the nine month time in the womb and then focusing on the first two years of our life, and after, is to keep it simple. So simple that everyone can understand what happened to us and from this understanding work to ensure no other addict like Sally is created and that every child will have what Robert had to get them through the constant trials and tribulations of life.

I am an addict because I lacked the materials with which to build a warm pot-bellied stove, the core of my soul, the place of comfort, calm and security to which people like Robert can turn, to get through the harsh cold realities that are life. Think of the warm pot-bellied stove, as the place we can huddle around to get warmth and comforting when we need it most.

I am not an addict because I had the materials with which to build that warm pot-bellied stove to get me through the harsh cold realities that are life.

This seemingly simple difference has made all the difference between us.

So read our stories. Embrace the pain I, Sally, will try to describe so you can first feel the trauma and cold before you can understand it.

Then, I, Robert, will describe the empathic nurturance I received. The materials with which I built the warm pot-bellied stove so necessary to cope with the harsh cold that is life. I want you to first feel, in my case, the warmth in order to understand how important it is.

SALLY'S STORY

The Past Shaping the Present

My parents come from very similar, almost identical backgrounds. The slight differences between them are primarily due to their gender.

My mom's parents both dropped out of high school in the first year. Not because they lacked the smarts to do the required work. They dropped out because their home environment was not supportive, encouraging or favourable to doing the work from which they could learn. There was very little peace in each of their homes, coming only at night or early morning when the adults passed out from sheer physical exhaustion or were in a drug or alcohol brought upon coma. There was much negative excitement in their homes. When all hell broke loose it usually started with verbal insults. There were threats, name calling and negative references to all that was a part of the other. Family intellect, physical appearance, competence, habits, even the smell of the other were insulted. Nothing was off limits. The fighting grew louder and louder and slowly grew from verbal insults to physical assault as alcohol or some other stuff was consumed.

Because my maternal grandparents were either under the influence, trying to get under the influence or in between, mostly feeling ill or hungover, employment was scarce. There was not much money and my mom mostly wore shabby hand-me-down clothes. Very early my mom knew she was different from the other kids. She was always told she looked different, smelled bad, had no food or unusual food to bring to school. Being with other children was mostly a negative, painful experience for my mom.

Home was no better. No one asked mom how her day was, what she did, what she learned or who she played with. At home mom was just a nuisance requiring some care, like being fed or on rare occasions having her clothes washed. She did not even have chores because that would have required acknowledging her existence and would have required some effort on the part of her parents to assign.

This was the routine, a familiar constant negative state, for my mom's youth and adolescence. Things never got better, in fact they only got worse especially when she went into puberty. Everything she learned about her body she learned from other girls. Girls who were similar to her. Girls who were also on the outside always looking in. Their school marks were poor and at home they all got shit but no guidance or help with anything.

My mom routinely got the same verbal and physical abuse my maternal grandparents dished out to each other. Except for my mom she had two abusers who targeted her several times daily.

The older my mom got the more she thought about running away. Escaping. But how could she have any confidence? So she only talked about it and as time passed it became her outsider group's main topic of conversation.

Since none of them had any confidence or sense of self-worth, my mom and her friends all believed that their ticket out could only be with a man. Until such a knight in shining armour came along they were happy to escape the harsh reality of their existence by doing whatever drugs or alcohol came their way.

The drugs or alcohol mostly came their way from boys similarly on the fringes and looking to score with any one of the girls.

My dad's story is similarly sad. In fact you could say their experiences were identical except in their behaviour. While my mom was shy and withdrawn my dad, as a typical guy, was very active and from the get go always getting into trouble. Teachers always said that he could do so much better if only he could sit still. He was always bothering the other children and was often given time outs.

My dad's teachers quickly learned that there was no point in calling his parents. They could care less and if they did, their only response was beating their son. So my dad learned first to put up with emotional pain then physical pain. It's no wonder he was frequently in fights and was not afraid of the pain involved in altering his body. He got several tattoos and piercings that made him stand out even from his group of similarly messed up boys.

His standing out from the rest was the attraction for my mom. She thought he must be brave and strong - just look at his ink and piercings - not to mention he was always in trouble with the tough guys he hung with.

Hooking Up, Having Sex and the Consequences

My mom and dad had a lot in common. Once they got past the physical part of their attraction to each other they could not stop talking about their own families. They even found humor in how their parents behaved often trying to one up the other by describing how bizarre their parents acted, swore and how, when stoned, they tried to assault each other. In short, how pathetic they were.

Both my parents completely lacked emotional and physical love. They were both starving for the warmth and powerful surge of feel good emotions that comes from touching. So they devoured each other physically. There was no holding back or holding out for either one of them. Kissing, quickly escalated to genital groping and then to out and out fucking.

Recently out of puberty, my mother had never taken a birth control pill and in their frenzy neither thought about a condom. She may have become pregnant the first time. There were many more times before my mom figured out that she was pregnant. It was no big deal, after all they loved each other judging from the frequent and incredibly pleasurable sex they were having. As well, the pregnancy was a great reason for leaving home and settling into a loving relationship with my dad. Or so she thought.

When my mom shared the news with my dad and her plan, he was right on board. He too believed the pregnancy was a blessing, saw it as the reason for leaving home and had, as joyful positive expectation as my mom had of their union. Both could not wait to share the good news with their parents.

They were shocked, when both sets of my grandparents responded most negatively. Sadly, my parents were very unrealistic about the response to Mom's pregnancy

My maternal grandparents called my mother a tramp and a slut accusing her of bringing shame on the family and their good reputation. They had long ago cut ties from the reality of their existence, their reputation and complete rejection of parental responsibility. To protect their imagined wonderful reputation my maternal grandparents insisted on a quick marriage before my mother's pregnancy with me showed.

My paternal grandparents' reaction was no different. They called my dad, a loser, especially for getting involved with a slut like my mother. Now my dad was sure to end up as a nobody and disgrace the good family name. a name which they, for no reason, believed to be highly regarded. In order to save their reputation they insisted that to make things right my parents had to get married immediately.

Both sets of grandparents bitched about the embarrassing behaviour of their children and agreed that there must be a marriage as soon as possible.

They called on a street chaplain who tried to help them when they were particularly bad off to perform the wedding ceremony. It was to take place in the recreation room of a friend. The food was planned to be two types of take out and a couple of cases of cheap beer.

There was no wedding shower, no bridesmaids or groomsmen and no baby shower to help my parents.

On their own, my parents searched for an apartment they could afford and could scrounge up enough money to pay for first and last month's rent. It was a very discouraging experience for them but eventually they found a place in a not-very-good part of town. The stink throughout the place was its most noticeable feature.

Furnishing for the place came from wherever my parents could get in cast offs from friends or cheap used items from some social service store. They were even able to find a not-too-beat up crib for me.

All of this happened before the end of my first three months in my mom's womb.

Moving into their own place was not a joyous occasion for my parents. They did it with the help of one of my dad's tough friends. In spite of my mom's efforts to clean she could not get rid of the stink. But like everybody else in the three story building both my parents got used to it and eventually could no longer smell it.

My parents decided that my dad would go back to an adult education program to finish his high school. The idea was to give him a chance to find a better job. In the meantime he would find temporary day jobs when not in class. My mom was going to work, as long as she could, for minimum wage or less.

These were difficult but hopeful times for my parents. The hope for a better life, than the one they left behind, however, did not last.

My mom was starting to gain weight and stopped caring about how she looked or smelled. Her smell started to blend with the stench of the building they were living in.

Needless to say most of the hot and enormously satisfying sex between my parents stopped almost as soon as they moved into their apartment. Not caring and using her pregnancy as an excuse my mom ate and ate and got fatter and fatter. To her credit, she stuck to her commitment not to drink alcohol or do any drugs while pregnant. She also kept all doctor's appointments although always going by herself.

Unhappy, disappointed, resentful and angry my dad went back to doing the only thing he knew to do. With his newfound friends at the adult education school, all in the same boat as he, and with his old tough-guy buddies he started to spend more and more time away from home. As they learned from their own fathers, their conversation mostly was about their ugly, fat bitch of a wife or girlfriend. To escape the constant negativity of their existence any and all mood-altering substances were consumed. Soon, at least for my dad, completing school fell by the wayside and he spent most of his sober time chasing after money to get high.

Paying the rent was increasingly difficult and responsibility for all household expenses fell to my mom. Her minimum wage part-time job was never enough. She was always behind paying one bill or another. My mom, from the very beginning of my awareness was always worried, unhappy and felt under attack. These feelings multiplied a hundred times as soon as my dad walked in the door. The negativity always steadily increased until both my parents collapsed out of exhaustion. It started up again immediately in the morning getting worse by each moment until my dad left. When he left my mom's negative state still continued but not as much and the entire pattern repeated every day, week and month. My mom was far worse off than when she lived at home. She was pregnant and had financial responsibilities, both of which she was ill-prepared to handle.

Now About Me

My very first feeling in the womb was that of an unpleasant need to quickly do something important. There was much to be done in a short nine months and it was my job to do it with the help of my mother. While I knew nature was taking care of most of my development I also knew that without my mom and me, my body, brain, senses and soul would not develop nearly as well as they could.

Almost at the same time as having this awareness I was very much aware of toxic conditions all around me and in me. I was feeling waves of tingling and stimulating heightened negative excitement and then periods of nothing. The nothing was not peaceful nor soothing. It was not warm or sweet. It was nothing and always short lived. The periods of excitement, the tingling, the heightened awareness, while at first invigorating, the contrast created an unpleasant experience of being jerked around. Soon the nothing periods melted away and all I felt was the sour and bitter taste that in part comes from being constantly tired out by always fearing the next negative sensation.

I came to know better the cause of the sour bitterness that was all around me and in me. It came from my mom who was reacting to her situation and the abuse she was receiving from my dad. When she tried to dish it back, which she often did, it made no difference to the sour bitterness I was constantly feeling.

I knew the stuff produced by my mom was bad and later learned its name to be adrenalin and cortisol. I also knew it to be a necessary part of me, a good part I would need sometimes. Knowing this did not make it less toxic to be constantly bathed in it. There was no bitter sweetness only sour bitterness in Mom's womb

Earlier I said my mom and I, together had in the womb life task of building me. While I had all the evolution-produced materials with which to build my organs and as a by-product my soul the constant presence of adrenalin and cortisol was like rain on a newly poured cement patio. With the adrenalin and cortisol rain nothing was as it could be. In spite of my natural drive to build my soul, where pot-bellied stoves reside, I could not.

It is truly amazing that I did not give up trying to accomplish my natural in-the-womb life task.

The closer I came to being born the more I felt that awful bitter sour taste made worse by the realization that a very critical task of the womb was incomplete. I was not ready to be born, but at the same time was eager to escape the toxic adrenalin cortisol environment created by my mom's circumstances. Part of me knew I was not ready and should stay. I settled for hoping anything outside of the womb would be better than inside of it.

I was very troubled by my inability to construct at least the pot-bellied stove frame. I had hoped the rest of it could be built with the materials produced by the love and care of my mom once I was born. Later I learned that people call this kind of good parenting, empathic nurturance.

Life Continues the Same as Before

My birth was traumatic and in the constant presence of cortisol. My mom was alone, no one but doctors and nurses to care for her. She did not know where my dad was, but guessed he was with his tough guy friends probably at the strip joint. She did not bother to call either set of my grandparents when she was ready. Why bother and add to her disappointment. She called a taxi instead. When she was ready to go to the hospital mom left a voice message for my dad. She knew he would not answer her call, although he could never resist answering any call that came in when he was with her.

Not ready but having to face the outside world I was immediately not a pleasant newborn. While I wanted to be soothed I could not be. While I was hungry and eager to taste the nourishment of my mother's milk, I could not. It had that same bitter sour taste I lived with in the womb and with it now came the stench of something rotting. My poor mom.

The physical touch of my mom's skin that I craved so much was not what I expected or needed. Instead of calming me, it felt cold and rough, literally irritating to my newborn skin.

Because my in the womb critical task was not even started I did not feel well and let it be known to everyone in the delivery room and any place close by.

Without even a frame of a warm pot-bellied stove I could not sooth myself. I felt exposed to a harsh cold world lacking any internal warming resources to ease the pain of my birth and the previous pain of my nine months in the womb.

This unpleasant pattern repeated every day in the hospital. What I remember the most from my first days was being hungry constantly for physical and soulful nourishment. I was desperate for my mom's milk but it made me sick. My stomach often hurt and often I could not stop myself from spitting it out. I could taste the same acidic bitterness in my mother's milk that I experienced in the womb.

The initial sense of urgency to get things done in the womb was changing and becoming more focused with nature. I had built my organs the best I could but I also knew some parts needed to be further developed. I was particularly aware that the work required to complete my brain was far from over and that in spite of my natural drive to build at least the frame of that warmth giving pot-bellied stove there were no materials with which to even begin constructing it. Thinking there was still time, I hoped the materials with which to build the heat-producing structure would soon be provided.

My hope for a better future was not to be.

My situation, our little family's situation, was not promising. It started with my mom's fearful unhappiness which produced that sour bitter adrenalin and cortisol substance. As part of my mom in her womb it was all around and inside me. Out in the world it was still there in her milk and in her being. Our problem was circular. My mom started out unhappy which made me unhappy which then made her even more unhappy.

I believed my dad was important and hoped that when we were home from the hospital he would come to our rescue. I especially hoped that by how he treated us that awful taste in my mom's milk would stop. Once it stopped I knew I would feel better. How could I not?

Home in Name Only

The simple act of going from the hospital to home was a continuation of the toxic negative sensations I experienced in the womb and in the hospital.

My dad did not get a proper infant seat for his rundown car so my mom's negative emotions flamed. She was particularly afraid. My dad's dismissing of her concerns only made her feel worse. Of course I felt the very same as my mom.

My first experience of home was the stench of the building. I could smell the stink even before we entered the front door. It added to the sour bitterness that was already so part of my existence.

When we entered what was going to be my home for a long time, the stench was not so bad but there was some very unpleasant bd feeling about it. I immediately knew this was not going to be a happy place for me or us.

The place was a filthy mess, so my mom told my dad. He did nothing but trash the place while we were in the hospital.

It was a struggle to feed me in spite of me being hungry. To my mom's credit she tried. As always the bitter sourness of her milk made my stomach ache and as much as I wanted to swallow the milk I could not help but spit most of it out. Eventually, with great difficulty, I fell asleep still hanging onto hope that my dad would rescue me and my mom. While I knew he did not when I was developing in the womb, I was still hopeful that things would be different now.

The sense of urgency, now a great deal more focused, only grew stronger. Not only was I very aware of the critically important life task of building that stove, I started to become increasingly aware of its absence. The feeling started out as an absence of warmth that was very real. It did not feel good. I sensed here was more to come of this bad feeling.

My immediate expectation of nothing but trouble, in this place called home started to come true. Quickly, we three settled into a very negative pattern. Hardly anyone came to visit. Once both sets of my grandparents met me at home, never in the hospital, they hardly ever came over. I knew when my mom had talked to her mom because her milk was more bitter than before. Thankfully shortly after my coming home mom decided to stop breast feeding. The formula was better. It was not sour or bitter. It did not make my stomach ache, and I no longer felt like I had to spit it out.

Unfortunately that problem solved was very quickly replaced by a series of daily negative experiences between me and my mom and then with my dad.

The world outside the womb is at the same time a very interesting and scary place. I was eager to explore everything but also easily frightened. As the absence of warmth started to gradually become a chill and later cold, I always felt upset and restless wondering and searching for what might decrease the unpleasant feeling. I was also frequently frightened. I hoped and expected that Mom would make me feel good about my explorations and comfort me when I became frightened. I also hoped and expected that she would be interested to get to know me as separate and apart from her with different likes, dislikes and interests. I knew if she empathically nurtured me I could eat this up and make out of it that warm pot-bellied stove I was really missing more and more.

My mom, sadly, could do no such thing. The reasons were many starting with her isolation from the outside world, absence of support from both sets of my grandparents and constant financial troubles. While I could no longer taste the bitter sour of her milk I sensed and I believe even smelled the constant presence of its cause, cortisol.

Nevertheless, I had not yet learned to give up hope and joyful anticipation of our relationship. When I wanted something, I joyfully anticipated that she would care enough to figure out what it was. In spite of not doing so, sticking a bottle in my mouth when what I really need was a change of diaper, I remained joyfully hopeful that the next time she would bother to think of me and not just make something up about what I needed. This seldom happened and when it did, it was simply by luck.

These were very painful experiences, mostly not to my body but to my sense of self. I did not feel lovable, or of any value to her. I felt like a heavy burden and a source of added unhappiness in her life. She said she loved me but I could feel no such thing. These experiences certainly were not the materials with which to build, what I increasingly knew to be, that all important and necessary stove in my soul.

The increasing coldness I felt and being treated as a burden by my mom was having a real harmful effect on me. I was slipping into an instinctive way of defending myself and preserving whatever opportunity remained to get the materials with which to build that warming stove.

Whenever I thought my life could not get any worse it did. Especially when I needed comforting. Upset and hyperactive, curious and exploring everything I was often frightened. Sometimes I physically hurt myself. The fear and hurt were minor and only important to me. Completely dependent on my mom and naturally expecting comforting from her on each occasion I would, with joyful anticipation, raise my arm to signal my need for a loving and assuring hug. At first they were seldom and later never forthcoming. This was at the core of our failed relationship, what people call a bond.

My survival as an infant, now around twelve months old, developed in a very clear-cut, completely instinctive way.

At first I cared about how mom responded to me, but slowly I stopped caring about her response and eventually I stopped caring about her. If there was a chance anyone else would be empathically nurturing I was open to it. There was nothing to lose and time was running out for building that pot-bellied stove. Besides the bitter coldness was getting to me more and more.

During the development, or the lack-of-development of a relationship with my mom, I was able to separate her from the person of my dad. As with Mom I was joyfully anticipating nurturance and comforting from him. I hoped from his empathic nurturance I could get the material with which to build that stove before it was too late.

There was no good reason, however, to be hopeful that my dad would rescue me or us. But I had not yet learned to expect very little, if anything at all, from him. Alone with my mom I was almost always alone with myself. She fed me and changed my diaper but it was always done quickly. There was no hugging, tickling or comforting. She barely spoke to me. At first, Dad was different. He did talk to me, held me, tickled and even hugged me. So you can't blame me for looking forward to his homecoming every night. The closer the time came, the better I felt. The few times he actually came home on time all the chilling cold got less intense. His presence even replaced the bad with an unusual good warm feeling that I waited for eagerly every night.

This happy experience did not last. No sooner did Dad get home and he paid attention to me for a while my mom and he would start arguing and then yelling at each other. The sweet warmth of his attention to me quickly faded every night. They yelled and argued with each other until I could no longer stand it. It always frightened me and when I discovered that sleeping stopped the fear, I no longer resisted the escape it brought me. I learned to let sleep take over. I also learned a very early lesson about escape that later became a significant part of my life.

Not that long into my early life, perhaps when I was fifteen months old, I started not to care, not to eagerly wait for that certain time for my dad to come home. It was a way of protecting myself to reduce at least one bitterness in my life. Whenever he came home was good enough. If he just acknowledged my presence, touched me in the slightest way it was good enough.

If the arguing and yelling between my parents produced the same bitter chill in them as it did in me, to protect himself, I guessed, my dad avoided coming home. Not only did he not come home at the same time, whenever he did come home he was almost always drunk or high on drugs. In that state there was no time for me. There was only time for arguing, hollering and sometimes pushing each other. Thankfully, I had already learned about escape through sleep. Instinctively, something else happened.

At first I looked forward to Dad coming home around the same time.

After many disappointments I did not care when he got home. In a very short time I stopped caring if he ever got home.

I suppose the feeling was mutual for my dad because just around when I turned two he stopped coming home altogether.

I did not care.

I continued not to care when Mom told me Dad was coming to see me, or to take me out. Sometimes, not often, he did come and even took me for a walk in my stroller. To protect myself it really did not matter if he did or did not. I was just as happy to see him or Mom as I was to see anybody who paid the least amount of attention to me. This included people when Mom was grocery shopping or the people at the doctor's office. People always said "What a happy friendly baby". Little did they know all I was trying to do was to escape, through any attention, the chilling cold to the bone that was my life.

Time was passing and knowing I had very little of it left to build that pot-bellied stove made my life even more miserable than it was already.

By my third year I was mostly with my mom. Physically she was getting increasingly less healthy, eating mostly junk food, smoking with me in the room and she started to drink alcohol more and more. By now she had made a few friends, other moms in the same situation as her. When not watching television she spent a great deal of time talking to them on the phone and getting together with them at the park when the weather was good. I, along with the other kids played on the park equipment with our moms watching a distance away. They talked among themselves and just let us play.

During this unsupervised play with other kids living the same life as me, I discovered another lesson in life, a lesson that would serve me well for a long time. I discovered another way of escaping the bitter chill-to-the-bone feeling.

My discovery at the playground was that if I was really fast at everything, if I ignored my fear and climbed to the highest point, if I jumped from the top and did all kinds of dangerous things, I no longer felt that bitter chill that was by now a constant in my life. So if I could not escape by sleeping, I escaped my horrible life through dangerous activity. The escape was so rewarding. I quickly learned the most dangerous and troubling way of doing everything. The escape was so complete that when my mom screamed at me to stop or to be careful I could barely hear it. Getting into trouble, being scolded was part of the escape and very rewarding.

The only time I could be still was during those few occasions when Mom told me Dad was coming to pick me up and take me out for something to eat. Although, by then I did not care if he came or not, just in case, looking for another brief escape from my feelings I patiently waited each and every time I was told he was coming. Sometimes he did but most often he did not. When he did it was like a big tease because it was so great, to be treated kindly, even if it was only for a short time. When he did not show up it was like having buckets of ice cold water, one after another, dumped on me. It did not matter though, because I stopped caring about him a long time ago and I was learning very good ways of escaping disappointments.

As soon as I knew, because it was dark and the street lights were coming on, that Dad was not going to show, I just revved things up. I went into super-speed mode, got into everything and all I could hear was "Sally don't do that.".

"Sally stop that.".

"Sally are you looking for a time out?".

"Sally I will count to three, one, two, three.".

I didn't care because being in trouble was just as good an escape as doing dangerous, risky things real fast.

I tired my mom out, I know because she always told me so. Both sets of grandparents, who seldom spent time with me, also said I tired them out. No one made me feel very good, at least not for long, and no one was eager or happy to spend time with me. The bone chilling-cold continued increasing little by little every day. But I had excellent ways of escaping it. The one, the first one, was sleep. The second, was to cause and to get into trouble. All the excitement created by both completely took my mind off the chilling cold that consumed my entire body.

Escape from Home

The trouble I caused and the trouble I was always in stressed out my mom to the point that not even her alcohol provided the escape she needed. She was desperate to get relief and was overjoyed when she found out I was eligible for day care and she could get financial assistance.

My first time at day care was filled with happy excitement. I recognized right away that there were many new opportunities in this place to cause and get into trouble. When Mom left me there I couldn't care less. I was eager to get going because the cold was continuing to get to me. The cold was not so bad when I got up but by the time breakfast was finished it always returned to the same level as it was before I went to sleep. As soon as Mom left the day care and left me with the teachers and other kids, I was desperate to escape my negative feelings and start the all-so-rewarding causing and getting into trouble.

Not surprisingly, my teachers at the day care started to say the same things as my mom and both sets of grandparents. I made them all tired.

The day care teachers told my mom there is something *wrong* with me. That she should have me checked out. That she should take me to a doctor to see what the physician had to say.

Labels People Put on You

Mom did just that the very next week. They talked about me causing and getting into trouble all the time. Mom gave many examples, coming up with another just when I thought she was finished. They talked for a long time about me as if I was not in the room.

At the end, the family doctor sent us to a specialist doctor who she said knows everything there is to know about badly behaved children.

It did not take long for Mom and I to see this specialist doctor. The very same talk took place in the specialist's office as it did with our family doctor. By then, my mom had more examples of me causing and getting into trouble.

I was about five years old when the adults in my life gave a sigh of relief. They finally knew what was wrong with me and how to fix it.

It turned out that my fast and dangerous causing and getting into trouble behaviour has a name. It is a very important name that only doctors can come up with. The special name, which everyone called me afterwards, was attention deficit hyperactive disorder (ADHD). Because, I caused and got into trouble, in spite of the adults always yelling, "Sally don't do that", the specialist doctor also had another name for my disobedient behaviour. He called it oppositional defiant disorder (ODD).

This was wonderfully good news for my mom, and both sets of grandparents. Finally, there were answers for them about me. Because the specialist doctor gave them official, important names for my bad behaviour and talked of a medicine for it, my mom and other people in my life now knew I had a medical problem. The fact that there was a medicine for it, confirmed that indeed I was sick.

What a relief for my mom, both sets of grandparents, my day care teachers and even my dad who very occasionally came around. All their and my problems would come to an end as soon as I started taking the medicine.

The medicine's name was Ritalin, something that was being taken by many other children with the same names the specialist doctor called me.

Since I only cared about a few things, sleeping and causing and getting into trouble to escape, I did not care about or resist taking the Ritalin pills.

It did not take long for the pills to make me feel different. The first difference I felt was an uncontrollable focus on one thing. I felt like I had no choice but to focus, stare at, one thing. This was very different from the energetic, on-the-go troubling way I behaved before.

At the same time, I became uninterested in everything around me. Before I was curious, interested in exploring my environment. Yes it got me into trouble, more often than not, but it was also a rewarding way of being. Because, on the pill I was focused on only one thing, the bitter, bone-chilling cold was not always present. Nevertheless I felt sad and drained of all the energy in my body. I felt numb and could not even laugh at my favourite television cartoon show. Mostly, I did not feel like myself.

What bothered me the most about this Ritalin *medicine* was that I could not escape into sleep as easily as before. Sometimes I could not fall asleep for a very long time. Lying awake, slowly the bitter, bone-chilling cold I felt less during the day crept in. To make my discomfort worse, I knew this was going to be my state for the rest of my life. The future, to me the afternoon, the evening, the next day, did not seem very promising as long as I was taking this Ritalin *medicine* and had no stove to warm my soul.

My mom, however, liked how this *medicine* improved her life. I was no longer causing or getting into trouble, she no longer had to frequently yell at me to stop doing something. Even the noise level in our home decreased. The teachers also liked how the *medicine* improved their life. They did not have to spend most of their time watching over me, stopping me from doing something risky and dangerous. Most importantly for them, I was no longer bothering the other children. Also, whatever I focused on, I learned far better than before. This turned out to be their reason for singing the benefits of the medicine.

In contrast to them, I hated feeling numb, lifeless, and especially feeling nothing like my previous self.

Fortunately for me, other people also started to recognize the absence of energy in my behaviour. My dad, the few times he came around, noticed the numbness and argued with my mom about the *medicine* I was taking. Like some others, he did not like what it was doing to me.

For several years I was on or off my *medicine*. Sometimes my mom would not give it to me on weekends, especially if we were going somewhere and she wanted to have me more lively. Sometimes she would not give it to me because my dad insisted on it, on the few occasions he took me out for lunch or supper. Often Mom would simply give in to me when I got fussy about taking it.

This jerking my body back and forth, taking the *medicine* not taking the *medicine* added to my not feeling well and my desperation to escape from it. By the time I was in elementary school, from grade six to grade eight, I was essentially off the stuff and primarily relying on lots of sleep and causing trouble as ways of escaping that always there, all-over, bone-chilling cold.

Hormones and Being a Sexual Being

When I started entering puberty, early around the age of ten, going on eleven, the constant not feeling well got even worse. I did not think it was possible to feel any worse but those new hormones sure did a job on me.

I just resorted to doing what I knew worked. Escape was certain the more trouble I caused and the more trouble I got myself into. By now the teacher's comments about me were like an old familiar song constantly going through my head. "Sally is so smart, she could do so much better, if only she focused, if only she paid attention, if only she did her homework". The theme always was the same. However, they were just words, because my teachers long ago had given up on me. My mom also gave up even nagging me about my behaviour, curfew and with whom I hung out. Talk of taking the Ritalin *medicine* also stopped long ago. By grade eight I was completely on my own, without any supervision, guidance or limits. Gradually I was becoming an almost invisible nuisance to my parents, grandparents and teachers. They could not be bothered with me. This kind of freedom was scary and just added to that constant nagging cold that ran through my body.

Happily, I was getting to be quite an expert at escaping that awful feeling. I was also learning new and better ways of doing it. Without intention or planning, a group started to form made up of girls similar to or just like me. We had much in common, especially feeling outside of it all. Even when we were physically on the inside, in a class, none of us felt to be in it. This was the base of a considerable bond among us. For the first time I did not feel alone. For the first time, there were people in my life who shared what I was feeling. They understood how I was behaving and why.

It was very easy to belong and to be accepted in this group. All that was required of me was to think and behave like the others in the group. The behaving included drinking alcohol, smoking pot and getting into trouble, mostly by hanging out with boys similar to ourselves.

Getting High on Anything

The first time I drank alcohol was in the spring of my last year in elementary school. I got more than just a buzz from it. I got relief from that nagging constant bone-deep cold with very little effort. All I had to do was drink. Even if I got sick, puked or had a hangover it did not matter. Quickly, I learned the fix would be there as soon as I could get that next drink. I sensed there were more wonderful surprises waiting for me. This made me even more curious and willing to take risks.

Much to my delight, I found the next best thing. It turned out to be better than alcohol. Pot was easy to obtain and very little of it produced an even better escape from what I was now calling *my shit life*. Pot also did not make me sick or give me a hangover.

I did not have to spend years in university studying and learning that we repeat behaviours that we experience as rewarding. Pot and alcohol, were especially rewarding. With very little effort and almost immediately, I was able to escape. Pot and alcohol were the answers to my dreams.

Since for a long time I had known that for the rest of my life I would have to live without the stove, that I could not make my own heat so necessary to apply my identified *smarts*, happily I discovered a way of escaping my fate. I did not need the life-enhancing warmth of the pot-bellied stove as long as I could escape the cold by getting stoned.

The absence of the warmth from within drove me to search for ways of escaping the cold. The earlier ways of getting into trouble required a great deal of work. The newfound ways did not. In short order, I became addicted to getting high. Whether the addiction was physical, mental or both, was not important. All that was important was getting to do it.

Romance or Just Having Sex

My early life experiences already prepared me not to care about virtually anything. Alcohol and pot took me to the next level. When high, whatever inhibitions I had were completely gone.

This made me very popular with the boys.

Somehow, I was passed or got promoted onto high school. I had no interest in studying, learning, fitting in or even thinking about let alone planning on a career. All I had interest in was escaping by getting high. And there were lots of opportunities for doing so, especially when the boys found out about the disinhibition effect on me.

By the fall of starting in grade nine I met Johnny. It was like this enormous powerful force was drawing us together. At first it was just his looks. Then as soon as we started to talk, he became mine and I became his answer to satisfying long unmet needs. Needs that were never satisfied when we were infants. Both of us had joyful anticipation of each other. We were the answer to our personal hopes and wishes for being accepted unconditionally, loved for just being who we are. When we talked, we had many things and interests in common. We both liked to escape the reality of our *shit lives* at first by causing and getting into trouble and later by getting high. There was much laughing about what we got into, especially when we started to describe our home lives. His parents were together mostly because they were too drunk all the time to leave. For the same reason, the worst they could do to each other was to hurl insults. Johnny said, which I thought was very funny, that most of the time he could not understand the insults because they slurred their words so much.

I told him about my separated parents and how they pretended to be important and acted as if they know everything. My mother was always telling her friends and parents what to do and was quick to criticize people for doing the same things she did. She drinks too much, Mom would say, as she was finishing her first cheap bottle of wine for the day. Johnny thought my dad was especially funny, introducing himself as mister and acting so self-righteous when he could not hold a job and contributed nothing to my well-being.

When we shared stories about our home life we always started out laughing and then ending the discussion on a sad note. We both wanted to escape and kind of talked around perhaps doing it together.

Then we discovered sex.

For the most part sex was new for both of us. We thought we knew some things but not really. However, we very quickly learned that kissing, touching each other, especially *the private parts* was incredibly satisfying. Compared to alcohol or pot, making out produced 100-plus percent satisfaction, escape from both of our *shit lives*. Because we mostly made out when we were high, we had no inhibitions about doing anything and everything, intercourse, fucking is what we called it, quickly happened. As our friends teased us, we were like rabbits. We could not keep our hands off of each other and we were always sneaking off to do it.

And It Starts All Over Again

Physically Johnny and I were in the prime of our lives. What we did not know, no one told or warned us about was that pregnancy for young people like us happens very easily. Probably I got pregnant the first time we fucked. When the pregnancy was confirmed, we excitedly considered it as our reason to escape our *shit lives* with our parents. We agreed to tell them right away and expected that they would, at the very least, help us set up our own place. Unrealistically, we thought they would be glad to get rid of us.

Instead both sets of parents were outraged by the news. Their good reputation, they said, was now ruined. My mom and dad, while separated, were together in saying they brought me up to be better than the slut I had become. Johnny's parents also were outraged calling him a loser who would never amount to anything, especially being with a slut such as myself.

To save their good reputation both sets of parents insisted that we must get married, to show everyone that their children were properly raised by proper parents.

There was nothing joyous about anything that happened after their outrage.

There was a quickly arranged marriage ceremony, a pizza and wings reception and a lot of beer consumed. Immediately after, we were sent on our way. Johnny and I paid a price for the ugliness of it all. No sooner did we move into our smelly apartment building then Johnny started to spend less and less time with me. Alone, most of the time, my mom and dad mad at me for ruining my life and theirs, I was in even greater need of escaping a far shittier life than I had before. For the baby's sake, I knew getting high was out of the question. It was, at that time, not an option. I could, however, eat and eat. I justified the eating by rationalizing that I was eating for two. As I got fat then fatter and fatter, Johnny had less and less interest in being with me and we even stopped fucking. Because he was seldom home, there was no fighting and stress, I had a pretty good pregnancy.

I did go to prenatal doctor appointments on my own and when it was time to have the baby, I went to the hospital in a taxi. Johnny was not around. One of his friends did find him and he showed up at the hospital while I was giving birth.

The birth went well, after all I was very young, and after some input from nursing staff, especially about breast feeding, they let us take our little boy home. We took him home in a taxi, Johnny holding him in a car seat. Probably not safe, but for the short trip it was good enough.

We had the basics for the baby but I was really *stressed* about what was waiting for me. I already knew Johnny was going to be little help and that I could not count on my parents. They were never there for me in the past, why would they be there for me now? So I settled into being, a more or less, single mom parenting a child that was not planned. But because of the pretty good pregnancy he was a joy to have. He was so sweet and so responsive to me. I felt, for the first time in my life, unconditionally loved. But like all honeymoons the bliss soon faded. The baby, probably sensing my stress, started to become difficult to nurse. The pleasure of feeding turned into discomfort then pain. Sleeping also started to be a problem for him. I was up with him throughout the night. Johnny never got up. Most of the time he was drunk or stoned.

Old negative feelings of bitter cold were emerging once the initial excitement of bringing home the baby faded. Escape started to preoccupy my mind. It didn't take much hinting on my part for Johnny to get it. Probably he remembered how *easy* I become when drunk or stoned. Alcohol was cheap and easy to get so one night after the baby went to sleep we got good and drunk and we fucked like the old days.

Too much booze and lacking practice consuming it, caused me to puke all night. I was in no shape to go to the baby when he cried, let alone feed him. Johnny had to attend to the baby but he had no idea what to do. He was really pissed.

That event, my first drunk after the birth of our son, put an end to breast-feeding him. It also put an end to my abstinence. The need to escape my new *shit life* was overwhelming and I knew, very well, just what to do about it. And I had company for the escape from hell. As before the pregnancy, Johnny and I were getting drunk or high very regularly. We returned to escaping the only way we knew how. Our son got fed and changed as he needed but I was very aware he was not getting cuddling, the attention and fussing I occasionally saw other moms give their babies. Guilt over this just added to thinking of my life as shit. Different from what it was with my parents, but nevertheless shit.

I feared the future was not going to be good. However, I could not help but to give into that need to escape regardless of the consequences. Already, by six months, the consequences for our son, were beginning to show. While he was *cared* for he seemed unnourished. Always hungry for nourishment and nurturance, I could not give him.

Everything started to look all-too familiar. A very distinct pattern was being repeated in front of my very own eyes. I saw the future of our son to be the past of my life and that of his dad.

If I could somehow deal with the coldness that was my life, perhaps I could make conditions better so my life, our life, would not be shit.

I knew I needed to get warm. Since it did not come from my inside, I knew I had to get it from the outside.

By then I knew people who were regularly attending Alcoholics Anonymous meetings. They didn't seem cold and they seemed to be dealing with shit in their lives far better than Johnny and I.

I felt out of control and for the first time admitted that I have a very serious problem. A problem I did not ask for but a problem I had to take responsibility for. If I did not look after myself I knew I could not take care of our son and that he too, would be sentenced to the same kind of life as me and his dad. The next evening, I was saying:

"Hi, I'm Sally and I'm an addict."

Everyone in the group responded:

"Hello Sally."

That evening was the beginning of the end to always feeling unbearably cold and the start of a new life for me and everyone I cared about.

ROBERT'S STORY

The Past Shaping the Present

My parents come from very different but at the same time very similar backgrounds. My paternal grandparents came from away and my maternal grandparents have lived in the same place for several generations. They each also come from different ethnic groups. What makes them similar is that both set of grandparents, in their own way, searched for meaning and purpose in their lives. They wanted to make things better, they wanted to make a difference in the world. For them the reason, why life was worth living, was very clear. Their way of achieving their purpose, was through positive relationships and deliberately developing the potential with which they were born. Both set of grandparents also believed that education, including skill training, can play a very important part in developing the potential with which everyone is born.

My father's parents, the new immigrants, came from a very troubled country in which opportunities for making life better were few and far between. In spite of considerable obstacles, both paternal grandparents completed the equivalent of post-secondary education. This was of considerable importance and played a part in being accepted as refugees, having something to offer their adoptive country.

As soon as they arrived, my paternal grandfather got a skilled labourer's job in a factory. My paternal grandmother stayed at home until my father started grade one. Until then, she focused all her attention on my father, keeping the house neat and clean and of course, cooking meals. My father got read to, was taken to places and every season, got a new set of clothes. There was not a great deal to be had, because only my paternal grandfather worked, but whatever they had was very nice.

Most importantly, both of my paternal grandparents believed it was important to take my father to places and events. They took my father to places just to see, to events to experience and to all sorts of family functions so that he had a very early sense of belonging. After everything there was always discussion. They discussed with my father what he liked, what he didn't like and why. As my father grew, he had lots to say as to what he wanted to see and experience.

One of the first things my father wanted was music lessons. He started before he even went to grade one. One or the other of his parents took him to music lessons and they shared responsibility for making sure homework was done and the required practising took place. Because the lessons started early in my father's life, he quickly became quite an accomplished piano player.

As soon as my father started grade one, my grandmother looked for and found good employment. Like her husband, she found a skilled labourer's position. In short order, she became a supervisor, which also improved her income.

Two incomes in the family made it even more affordable to expose my father to experiences through which he developed, especially his thinking potential. Most importantly, my father's curiosity grew by leaps and bounds. He was curious about everything. My grandparents encouraged and supported the curiosity. They bought my father books and a computer on which he could research his interests. Since curious people are good learners, not surprisingly, my father was a top-notch student. This pleased his parents to no end and was the reason for continuing to do what they had been doing, but more so.

It was important in my father's parents' home to have balance between work and play. Both grandparents followed this rule for themselves and taught it to my father as well. They also believed in boundaries and, within limits, allowed my father to make choices. As a result of their relationship, trust and respect, virtually everything was discussed and any and all learning opportunities were taken, discussed and as a result were a great benefit to my father's development.

In many ways, my father was the centre of attention of his parents and his extended family. It was not overwhelming, however, and he never felt like his parents were constantly hovering over him. He did feel loved and important to his parents and their interest in him and what he was doing reinforced this positive feeling.

My father's home was a true sanctuary in which everyone shared responsibility for keeping it that way including following a well-thought-out division of labour.

When Father started pre-school he had already learned how to play and share with other children. Meeting new children, was a continuation of positive experiences from the past and he looked forward to spending time with his new friends every school day. The teachers described him as a joy to have in the classroom, often sharing with his parents how helpful he is with the other children and them. I guess because he was so comfortable in his own skin, after all he had his warm pot-bellied stove, he was able to successfully do whatever was asked of him. This pattern continued into elementary school, including how well he was regarded by both his teachers and fellow students.

Almost from the start, my father's parents focused on what was the right and wrong thing to do. As to be expected, my grandparents did not tell him the answer. Instead, the answer was discovered through discussion. At some stage my grandparents introduced another idea into their discussions. When the difference between doing the right and wrong was pretty clear, at least about not very complicated things, they started talking about "what is the good or fair" thing to do.

You might think that all this discussing and talking was too much. You might think that it would sooner than later bore a young person. On the contrary, since the talking and discussing was done with empathic nurturance it was key to the development of the potential with which my father was born.

By the time Father got to high school, all the teachers described him as "mature for his age". Mature, because of his responsible behaviour, attentiveness and ability to whatever was required of him. To behave in this way Father had to feel good, which he did because there was a comfortable warmth in his core.

He had that pot-bellied stove and the warm comfort it provided allowed him to apply himself to the task of learning. There were others like him and they were drawn to each other. As they all learned to do at their respective homes, they talked and discussed everything. They learned from each other and inspired each other to search for meaning and purpose to their life. These were high school students who already were figuring out why life is worth living. They just had to work on the *how* of doing it.

Because this group of students' marks were good the school encouraged them to participate in sports. There were lots to choose from and as soon as they got involved, each began to realize that the involvement represented at least one way of living a life that had purpose and meaning to it.

There were other ways available in school for finding meaning and purpose. Student council, debate club, charitable functions and areas of choice in which to volunteer, were others. My father and his group of friends looked forward to the next day every day. They genuinely liked their life. Talk of the future became increasingly more frequent as the end of high school was quickly approaching. All his friends, male and female, planned to attend post-secondary educational facilities.

My mother's story is very similar to my father's. Her people were long-time residents but certainly immigrants through and through. They were proud of their heritage, but a long time ago stopped referring to themselves by the place which they left behind.

Slowly but steadily, my maternal grandparents' people bettered themselves and their economic situation. Each generation accomplished just a little more, taking full advantage of the opportunities life presented. My maternal grandfather was a registered professional as was my grandmother. Both read lots and tried very hard to behave responsibly. This very much included parenting. Since a baby does not come with instructions, they made it their business to get a *manual* before they brought my mother home from hospital. In fact, they bought two manuals so they could each read chapters at the same time and then discuss the rationale and strategies for parenting. They actually made up a parenting policy of their own, agreeing that their behaviours, alone or together, would always be guided by it. My grandparents saw parenting to be what it is, the most difficult and challenging task they would ever have to do in their life.

They took parenting seriously.

What they learned from their parenting *manuals* were very basic strategies, policies as hey called them. They didn't have to be taught to empathically nurture my mother. That came easily for them. It came easily because both of them received it from their parents when they were infants. They knew, their infant daughter, my mother, was a separate, uniquely different person from them. Recognizing this reality motivated them to learn how their infant signalled her needs and what her needs were. This is good construction material with which to build a pot-bellied stove.

My grandparents also learned what efforts promote growth and development and did as many of them as they could. Like my paternal grandparents, they deliberately planned, many different experiences for my mother. Then, they too discussed and debriefed each other afterwards.

As you would predict from the brief description of the environment to which my mother was exposed when it came for her to start school she took to it like a duck to water. She loved interacting with children and engaging in the various group and individual activities. In elementary school, learning one thing was such a fantastically positive experience for my mother, she could not wait to learn the next thing. She loved school and school loved her. Without being consciously aware of it, very early in her life, my mother was being taught and she was learning why life is worth living. At the very same time, she was being taught how to live it.

My mother could not wait to start high school. She was not worried about making new friends, after all, she had already learned how to make and keep friends. She was not worried about school work, homework or other academic challenges. She already knew that learning new stuff is incredibly reinforcing. She also knew that creating new ideas from putting together a bunch of different ideas was especially fun.

Puberty, and the raging hormones that come with it, for both my parents, was a natural life event that was not only acknowledged but also quietly celebrated. Their respective sexuality was treated as a very positive developmental stage to welcome, rather than one to ignore or to be embarrassed about. Both got good information about the physical changes in their body, as well as about responsibilities that come with it. This was a very good time in my parents' life, although not without some difficulties. After all, they were still teenagers figuring out how to live life.

Eagerly my mother explored and involved herself in all sorts of extracurricular activities in high school. She played sports, belonged to social clubs and made many friends in the process. Her group of friends, diverse in every way, had one important thing in common. As they got close to graduation, they increasingly talked about and planned their future. They knew that anything sustainable and worth having requires effort and time to achieve. While plans can and do often go off track, they knew that without one, very little can be accomplished.

Consequently, plan they did and when the time came did what was required by it.

Hooking Up Slow and Steady

My parents met each other when they were seniors in high school. She was part of his group of friends. The friendship became more when the graduation prom was in the not-too distant future. Neither of them was looking for a romantic relationship. They were enjoying life just fine without one. Practicality and social custom required, however, a compromise to which all the group gave in. They could have all gone to the prom as a group, but after discussion, decided it was more practical to pair up. If for no other reason than to know for what girl the guy was buying the corsage.

Initially, the romance of my parents was anything but hot or intense. It was very casual, but pretty steady during the summer after graduation. At the end of the summer, my mother and father went to different post-secondary places of education. In fact, they went into school residences in different towns. While very exciting and totally fulfilling experiences for both, by the end of their casual dating during the summer, they were more than less committed to each other. They promised to see each other during the school year whenever the opportunity presented itself.

They were not in a hurry.

Being separated was not an emotional hardship for either one of them. It was part of their plan. It was also part of their plan when, where and how they would get together during school semesters, holiday breaks and summer time.

What they did not plan was the course of their romance. It was just a happy by-product of their planning. The physical aspects of their romance also progressed gradually. Neither my father nor my mother was in a hurry about the physical stuff. It was as if they wanted to savour every part of it. All the physical aspects were emotionally based and focused on conveying care and respect for the other. Not that they never experienced some raw erotic stirrings, after all they were in their youthful prime. They were nevertheless very much aware of the pitfalls that came from deviating from their plan. There was no need to be in a hurry for intercourse. While they wanted to do it, they agreed to wait for the right time. In the meantime, what they physically did to express their love for each other was fun enough.

The Christmas before graduation my father, from his four years of summer work savings, bought an engagement ring. He planned and proposed to my mother on New Year's Eve. She was delighted and joyfully accepted.

On New Year's Day, with both sets of parents together, who by then had become social friends, my father and mother announced their engagement. It was happily received and there was much celebration that day.

Before the end of the New Year's Day and the engagement celebration my parents and grandparents predictably went into full-scale planning mode. The wedding date was set eighteen months later. My parents wanted to complete at least one year of employment after their graduation in their respective fields. They planned to be able to purchase a starter home by then. Until then they would continue to live at home and save.

Eighteen months simply flew by because of all the activities. There were graduation celebrations to be had, there were securing employment celebrations, then wedding plans to be made, a honeymoon destination to decide, bridal showers, a bachelor party and last, but not least, a starter home to purchase. Because there was a plan, everything got done more or less on schedule.

On their honeymoon, my parents made full love, intercourse, for the first time. For them, waiting made sense and it worked. It was tender, caring, slow and sensual for both. As a result their making of love got better each time.

An important conversation, having to do with my future conception, took place during that special time away after the wedding. True to their form, they planned what both my mother and father recognized to be the most important decision of their life. Making a baby. After much discussion, at which they were quite skilled by then, a time was set for having me. Until the time for conception, they decided my mother and my father would use birth control methods.

I know it sounds all too perfect but my parents were schooled planners, and life had taught them the benefits of doing so. While they enjoyed making love, once they started, the actual time to conceive was like a well-orchestrated military campaign. My mother went off the pill to coincide with her ovulation cycle and, as they say, they got busy.

My Life

Soon enough, with youth and health on their side, *they got* pregnant. After waiting for the first three months, my conception was announced first to the family then to friends. It was received with much delight and great celebration at which, especially, both sets of grandparents were very good.

Once the parties were was over, everybody went into action. There was much to do. My parents signed up for Lamaze prenatal classes and both attended visits with my mother's obstetrician. One of the smaller bedrooms became my designated nursery. There was painting and decorating, all gender neutral, my parents preferring not to know my gender until I physically showed myself.

Of course, there were also a number of baby showers, put on by both sides of the family and by my mother's bridesmaids from the wedding.

It was a joyous, busy time.

It was a joyous time too for me in the womb. My first experience of life was a soothing wash of sweet smelling warmth. I felt incredibly safe and comfortable. Just when I thought it could not get any better, it always did. Those extra special times always were associated with events in my mother's environment. When my dad got home from work was one of the times. Early, I learned to look forward to his homecoming. When my grandparents visited were some of the other times. There were many other visits that my mother enjoyed, judging from the positive physical effect she passed on to me.

Even when alone, when Mother was reading one of her many parenting books she passed on to me her sense of well-being that I experienced as sweet-smelling warmth. Life was good in the womb and I had plenty of material with which to start building one of life's greatest task, my soul and the frame of my pot-bellied stove that resides in it.

I must admit that the prospect of being born was not appealing. In spite of having no reason to worry about the actual physical birth, because my parents were fully prepared, what with all the classes and doctors' appointments, I did not want to leave the familiar comfort of the womb. I was completely ready in nine months, however, and there was no delaying the inevitable. I had successfully built all my organs, all the intricate vascular and neural connections, the size and state of my brain was what it should be and most importantly I had the basis of my pot-bellied stove to build upon once I came out into the world.

Home is Where the Heart Is

My reluctant feelings about being born disappeared as soon as I felt my mother's naked chest and tasted her sweet, warm nourishing milk. As always, my father's presence just made Mother and I feel even better than when we were alone.

There was much excitement and work involved when it was time to go home. Flowers, cards of congratulations, and especially, me, had to be transported home. Father got an infant car seat and Mother sat beside me in the back on the way home. My room was a bright, happy place decorated with a lot of stuff, I had difficulty fully appreciating, after all my infant eyes were just learning to see. What I could not clearly make out I felt. It was a very good feeling.

At the hospital and at home, Mother and Father both agreed to work very hard at getting to know me for who I am. They listened to my signals and interpreted their meaning increasingly better day by day. Very quickly I was very much aware that they *get me*. They easily recognized what I was communicating and met my simple needs exceptionally well. While they tried some parenting techniques about sleeping and eating patterns, most important for me was that they *got me* and used that understanding to respond to me. I loved that empathic nurturance, ate it up and with what I was metabolizing, I was slowly but surely building the rest of my warming pot-bellied stove.

Mother and I soon settled into a comfortable routine. For the first while I was pretty much constantly hungry, especially at night. Sometimes my mother came to get me, sometimes it was my father. Nursing always was a very wonderful experience. I was devouring my mother's milk, digesting it fully and its sweet nourishment provided more materials with which I continued the life tasks required of me.

I knew from the start that I was important and much loved by all my family. It was a wonderful feeling.

At worst, when Mother and I were alone, while Father went off to work, I could sense that she got tired. It was mostly in the afternoon or at the end of the day. In the afternoon, one or the other set of grandparents came to help. This was a time of great joy for me because they were so attentive. I also could sense the relief my mother felt when they came to visit. Even better for my mother and I was when Father came home from work. Almost always, he came home at the same time. We both looked forward to his happy announcement "I'm home".

I don't know what father did at work but I do know that he never complained nor did he act tired when he got home. He helped mother with everything including feeding after I stopped nursing. Father also did his share of changing my diapers.

Around the age of two, when I was supposed to be terrible, I was not. I believe this was because by then I had fully constructed that all-important warm stove that calmed me from within.

My mother had many friends and they visited regularly with their own children. While the mothers watched us and chatted we played. It was a great deal of fun and we liked each other's company. By the time I started attending at a cooperative day care, I was ready not to be with my mother all the time. Also, I was ready to play with the other children. I learned to be cooperative, mostly this involved sharing, when it was time to learn it so I would never forget it.

All the good things that were happening to me, the way people other than my parents treated me, added up to an overwhelming feeling of being lovable. This, with my warm pot-bellied stove, made me ready for the world outside of my home and the cooperative day care where mother was often present. Day care was a very positive fun time for both me and my mother.

Making sure that my first day at grade one would be a success Mother walked me to the school before I was scheduled to start. She introduced me to the man and lady who would be my teachers and let me watch the children play during recess. I could not wait to start school and eagerly looked forward to it.

September came soon enough and when Mother said goodbye at the school door I entered feeling good about the new experience. The warm glowing stove inside me and having learned that I am a loveable child were the main reasons for having this good experience. Learning and exploring, having my curiosity encouraged, working and playing with other children all produced positive consequences. All I had to do to continue to feel good, or even better, was to continue to behave in a positive manner. Mother was told constantly "Robert is such a good boy. He is such a pleasure to have in class. He gets along so well with the other children. He likes to help and he is such a good learner". This made Mother and Father feel very good, which in turn made me feel even better. They were proud of me.

As to be expected elementary school went well, as did the summer holidays, which were divided between just family time fun and fun learning. After each summer holiday, I did not dread going back to school nor the challenges of the coming year. With experience-earned-confidence I looked forward to what lay ahead.

Not surprisingly, I also did not dread the new experience of starting high school. I actually looked forward to making new friends and carrying on with the old friends from elementary school. Family, friendships and learning all combined to create a good life. I looked forward to every new day while thoroughly enjoying the moment. I was on the inside and I liked it.

High school also provided new opportunities to explore student activities, sports and other ways to grow and develop my potential. I joined the drama club and played a couple of intramural sports. I tried to balance my school work with fun, an ambition that was supported and encouraged by my parents and grandparents. The four years passed very quickly, as did the summer school breaks during which I started to learn about work for pay. Since I liked to learn and a long time ago I learned that working has its own rewards, imagine the joy of discovering that at the end of every two weeks I actually got paid hard cash for doing what I liked.

And It Starts All Over Again

My close group of friends in high school was made up of girls and boys and we just all hung out. Graduation was a problem because we had to make a decision about how to go to the prom. After much discussion, a practice I learned well from my parents, and some good-natured teasing, most of us paired up as dates for the prom. My date, as it turned out, was to be my future bride.

By the time of the prom, we both knew to what post-secondary educational facilities we were heading. As luck would have it, they were in different cities. Talking about our future careers during the summer brought us closer together. By the beginning of the post-secondary school year, we considered ourselves to be a couple and discussed at length how we would keep our relationship alive and well despite being separated by distance for a good part of the year.

It would be wrong to leave out that as our relationship grew, so did our physical attraction to each other soar. We discussed this part of our togetherness and with difficult determination settled on waiting for intercourse. Knowing that this was a difficult decision for both of us made it somehow easier.

This commitment was especially difficult in the summer months when we were home from school and saw a great deal of each other. It was during my last school year break summer job that I decided to buy an engagement ring and propose on New Year's Eve.

But wait, you heard all this before.

REFLECTIONS

About Sally and Robert

A long time ago, and the hard way, I learned to avoid such words as invariably, always, never and truth. While I tentatively hang on to using the words fact or empirical evidence, I readily concede that there are exceptions to any described phenomenon or category of events. The stories of Sally and Robert are composite life histories I have heard over 48 years of practice and an equal number of years of reading to better understand the human condition.

While on the topic of words, in writing Sally and Robert's stories every effort was made to be true to their voice. To tell their stories as they would speak. The intent was to make their stories easily readable and even more importantly believable.

In this debriefing discussion section I have exerted effort to tone down my voice to be less formal and more consistent with the preceding two sections. In spite of my genuine effort in this regard you might still have to reread some sentences and very occasionally, I hope, consult your hard copy or online dictionary. Sorry about that.

One of the several reasons for writing TWO is to help the decision-making process of those who are trying to figure out how life has shaped them to become who they are now. Specifically, in part it is written for those who have control problems over whatever they do excessively. That can be substance abuse, gambling, eating excessively or being addicted to love, as so well sung by Robert Palmer many decades ago. As is all-too-well-known by most, there can be no end to the list of messed up patterns of behavior in which one can engage.

Needless to say the stories of Sally and Robert are deliberately simplified to make a point. There is a recognized and accepted problem with this approach. The problem is that it readily affords, for those so inclined, to wiggle out of the reality of their life. One can easily cherry-pick contradictions with their own life story and rationalize their ongoing dysfunctionality. For example, one can say my mom did not get fat or my dad did not leave us so the story does not apply to me. State of the art treatment centres are designed to address this kind of skirting of reality as well as the child like creations of pleasing fantasies, especially about one's early life experiences. In spite of the loopholes provided by the way the stories of Sally and Robert are told, I firmly believe that in the heart of hearts, each reader will know whether they have or have not a warm pot-bellied stove.

Similarly, those so inclined to stubbornly hang on to a medical model of what it means to be an addict, or those who feel the need to continue to believe in the hereditary gene explanation, in their heart of hearts they too will know that it is not a medical problem or a genetic predisposition. They also will know that in their families addicts are being created from one generation to the next and that the consequences of doing so are far and wide ranging. The decision required of us all is how much we continue to fund the industry that reacts to the consequences of creating addicts or better fund preventative measures and eventually eradicate the current use and abuse of alcohol and drugs.

Being an Addict and Becoming Addicted

An addict is a *made person* rather than a born one. Because of adverse environmental conditions, during gestation and the first two years of life, the person lacks the materials with which to construct a warm pot-bellied stove. This makes the person very different from those who have one.

Alligators provide a great analogy. They are one of the oldest living creatures on this planet. They are magnificent creatures with an intense innate instinct to survive. In spite of this, they cannot survive without an external source of heat because they are cold-blooded. They are not bad, wrong, or defective because of this. They simply are. Similarly, addicts, people without a pot-bellied stove, are not bad, wrong, or defective because they cannot live (stay abstinent) without an external source of heat. They simply are. As such, both the alligator and the addict have to live in harmony with this reality.

An addict therefore, is different in a very special way: a way that is characterized by a pervasive, intense discomfort, not unlike being without proper attire in the freezing cold. As illustrated, an addict, like Sally and her mother, is driven to escape the discomfort. It is accomplished in different ways at first and then eventually by ingesting substances that alter physiological and emotional states. Because the consequences of ingesting a *drug* is so rewarding, the addict becomes intensely driven to repeat the behavior. It does not take long, or many successful escapes from one's shit life, to become addicted to substances and the physical, emotional and psychological effects they produce.

All addicts, sooner than later, become addicted. As told by one addict, "I had my first taste of escape as soon as I was able to carry a beer bottle".

An important distinction to make, and a very serious social issue that deserves its own separate treatise, is that anyone can become addicted. Even people with a warm stove churning out heat inside them. The route for such people to become addicted has many paths. Alleviating pain caused by acute or chronic medical conditions are the most familiar. Concussions and the collateral damage they do to the endocrine system, so aptly described by Lawrence Komer (2016) is another significant pathway.

The fact that we are social creatures and that we are stuck at the tribal or reference group stage perspective (Polgar 2009) is probably the major pathway to addiction. Because of the need to belong, it does not take long for a pot-bellied stove individual to become addicted to any array of substances used by the group to which the person wants to belong. For example, a new employee in a certain occupation eagerly joins established colleagues for a pint at their *club*. One pint becomes two, one night becomes two, and the next thing you know, the new person is having several pints every working night and even more pints on weekends. There is no need to elaborate on the physiology and psychology of slowly habituating the body and mind to a new status quo. Suffice it to say it does not take long for even a pot-bellied stove individual with an ill-advised need to belong to become addicted.

To reiterate, TWO is less about becoming addicted and more about the making of an addict. It should be noted, however, that eventually, almost all addicts, sooner than later, become addicted.

Life is Complex But Not Always to the Same Degree

Robert's story is considerably shorter and by comparison simpler than that of Sally's. The difference is not deliberate nor intended to convey that Robert's parents, indeed his own life, did not have its share of trials and tribulations. Compared to Sally's, however, Robert's story is markedly less complex. The lesson is that doing what is functional is easier than not doing it. The challenge for Sally's family was knowing what to do, which clearly they did not. Moreover, they did not know what to do intergenerationally. The empirically supported contention is that this is not about bad genes, a gene for being an addict. Instead, the premise is that environmental conditions, along with some innate propensities determine whether or not we can make a pot-bellied stove with what we get.

By virtue of the family into which Sally was born, by the age of two she was destined/programmed to be an addict. She was also destined to have her innate cognitive developmental potential obstructed. By virtue of the family into which Robert was born, he was destined to a different future.

Needless to say, the deterministic impact of environment and our responsibility for creating it is not palatable, so we settle on a genetic explanation. It serves to absolve familial, cultural and social responsibility. We need to reclaim the importance of environment because it is within our power to make that better. This is one of the important messages of TWO.

For those who insist on the genetic explanation, the challenge is to find empirical evidence in support of it. As of the date of this writing none has been forthcoming. Moreover, there are a good number of sound empirical studies against the genetic argument, including debunking studies of twins. Good places to start examining the arguments against the genetic/medical model would include, but are not limited to, the writings of Gabor Maté (2008), Duncan and Miller (2000), Conrad and Schneider (1992), Read, Mosher, and Bentall (2004) and Montcrieff (2009). As you can see from the dates of these publications there is nothing new about the two sides in this debate. What is disconcerting is that in spite of the lack of evidence, most of the world, aided and abetted by psychiatry, stubbornly hangs onto the genetically inherited explanation. At the very least, now we better understand the appeal of this medicalization of an environmentally induced non-organic problem. Even if we tentatively accept that there is a gene responsible for a person being an addict, surely that gene would have to be environmentally activated.

Temperament

Undeniably we are all born as unique beings. This includes our temperament. As such, some infants need more attention and nurturing than others and some are content and can thrive on very little. Another child raised in as an adverse environment as Sally possibly could have used the little she received as material with which to build that all important, part of the soul, the pot-bellied stove. Another child in as ideal of a home as Robert, because of innate temperament, could have experienced all the empathic nurturance and parental attention as inadequate. That child, to the astonishment of onlookers, possibly could be *programmed* to be an addict and behave as such, becoming addicted early in life.

While these are remote occurrences they are nevertheless possibilities.

To prevent even the remotest possibility of a Robert being programmed to be an addict a critically important temperament propensity type requires examination. Years ago, Elaine N. Aron (1996) wrote about a group of people she characterized as *highly sensitive*. The characterization and descriptions were innovative and served to explain the difficulties of children who otherwise would have been expected to thrive without any difficulties. Unfortunately, the idea fell out of fashion or more accurately never really made it into the mainstream, although it was a national bestseller. Currently, few people, especially parents, know about this temperament type.

While there is no robust data as to how prevalent this highly sensitive innate temperament is, based on my clinical experience I believe it to be very common. We could do far worse therefore, than to *assume* every child, meets the criteria to be classified as a highly sensitive person. If we all assume this about each and every child we would be extremely motivated to understand the implications of the classification, especially when it comes to how to optimally empathically nurture a child.

To do this approach justice, Aron's book should be mandatory reading for all parents and should be one of the most important texts in a family's parenting book library. It should be noted here that Robert's parents bought and read several *child care manuals* whereas Sally's parents had none.

As with all conceptual frameworks (including TWO) the notion of a highly sensitive person is not without some contentious components. For instance, was Sally difficult to feed because she was reacting to mom's stress or would have been difficult to feed regardless of mother's state because she is a highly sensitive person? Or is it both? The premise is that it does not matter. What matters is that knowing about the temperament should suffice to assume that every child is highly sensitive and should be parented accordingly.

Choices or Compulsion

We are fond of or in the habit of invoking and indiscriminately applying the concept *choice*. We say about badly behaved people, especially addicts, that they are making a choice, implying a bad one at that.

Sometimes we will allow that the choice is an ill-informed one albeit something the person should know better than not to make.

This paradigm applies in a very limited way to an addicted addict.

To illustrate this point, I often use the story of two young braggarts trash talking about how tough each one is. The talk takes place in the dead of winter, thirty below zero, at the farm of one of the tough guys. The other lives some distance away and brags that he can walk home without his extremely warm insulated parka to his beautiful, loving wife and two darling children.

Leaving the parka behind he starts his journey in the freezing cold and blowing blizzard. The tough guy gets a little disoriented and the walk is taking longer than expected. Slowly, he begins to lose core body heat and gradually transitions into an involuntary freezing-to-death process. In spite of having a great deal to live for, in spite of his promise to be home soon, he dies.

This tragic story is not unlike what happens to the addict without the pot-bellied stove or the alligator that is exposed for a period of time to freezing temperatures. The alligator freezes to death. The equivalent to freezing to death for the addict is to use a substance with which to escape the insidious prevailing constant bitter cold that characterizes, as for example, Sally's life.

In the story and in life, death or using is not a matter of choice. Both are involuntary processes. As the alligator freezes to death involuntarily in the freezing cold so too the addict involuntarily uses to escape the blizzard that is his or her life.

The only choice for the alligator is to stay close to the equator. The only choice for the tough guy is to wear the parka. The only choice for the addict without the ability to warm from within is to get external heat with which to *stay alive*. More about the source of that external heat later.

Solutions

There are two strategies for addressing this tragic occurrence of creating addicts who become addicted like Sally. The first and best strategy is to avoid/prevent it from occurring in the first place. It involves, deliberately, in a concerted manner, breaking the intergenerational perpetuation of this dysfunctionality. Elsewhere, the strategies required to accomplish this improvement in the human condition are described at length (Polgar 2009). Realistically, it will take several generations to complete the transformation, but, it can be done.

The doing involves learning about romantic attraction and choosing an adjusted, developmentally advanced partner with whom to procreate. The second critical doing involves learning about empathy and parenting with nurturance that is empathic. When done consistently well, the child will ingest and metabolize the empathic nurturance and make out of it their warm pot-bellied stove.

This preventative strategy also can and does avoid a great deal of later-life string of negative tragic consequences.

The second strategy does not create a pot-bellied stove where there is none. It does, however, prevent going into the involuntary freezing to death (relapse) process. Both the alligator and the person without the internal warming core need an external source of heat. What the external source of heat is continues to be debated. The late Amy Winehouse sang about *Rehab* and thereby the mainstream thinking of intervention as rehabilitation. In this way of thinking there is no distinction made between the addict and the addicted. Returning one to some former state, which is the definition of *Rehab*, is a medicalization of a non-medical problem. Instead, a relevant intervention has to address the absence of a pot-bellied stove. Moreover, in this way of thinking there is no distinction made between being an addict and being addicted. Not all addicted people are without pot-bellied stoves. The intervention they need therefore is very different.

The unofficial, not empirically proven, but experientially supported best (and only relevant) external source of heat required by addicts is that which comes from the Alcoholics Anonymous fellowship. It does not come from religion, the love for a child or spouse, career, oaths, promises or strength of character. There are religious people, contentedly married family people, people with great careers and fierce strength of character all in need of AA's external heat. We know this because they are in the twelve-step program.

The amount of external heat required by an addict can also depend on circumstances. It was too many years ago to remember exactly when Little Mike taught me a very valuable lesson about surviving blizzard conditions without an internal heat source. As long as he was working on a particular project with a particularly *nasty* individual Little Mike survived the freezing cold by attending an AA meeting in the morning and one at night every day. When the project ended, and the extraordinary freezing blizzard was over, he returned to his four times a week meetings.

While AA experientially presents as the only viable external source of heat for people without a pot-bellied stove. There is much wrong, or at the very least, outdated about how it is conceptualized. Because the silent partner of the two founding individuals was a physician, a psychiatrist to be specific and Bob, one of the founding partners, also was a physician there is much inappropriate medicalization of a non-organic based problem. Consequently, medical jargon is used. Moreover, by its very name the program is all about alcohol instead of the underlying problem of being an addict because one does not have a warm pot-bellied stove. Conrad and Schneider (1985) more than 30 years ago very extensively discussed this problem. The conceptual problems prevail, however, probably because those who accept their need for the program *get over* the difficult issues, and learn to live with them, since they are getting what they really need – the external source of heat and the life that comes with it.

Acceptance

The first step in the AA twelve-step program is: "We admitted we were powerless over alcohol – that our lives had become unmanageable."

As in addressing any problem, the first task is to accept that there is a problem. Notwithstanding the singular focus on alcohol, for many, accepting the problem of abusing alcohol while necessary, it is insufficient. It is insufficient because the focus on alcohol distracts from a focus on a much greater life enduring condition. The absence of a pot-bellied stove. A condition for which there is no cure as there is no cure for that proverbial alligator which also cannot live without an external source of heat.

It would not be unreasonable to, at the very least, hypothesize that understanding the underlying nature of being an addict would make it easier to accept being one. More importantly, no one but the person can evaluate or determine the presence or absence of a warm pot-bellied stove. Only the person can compare their experience to the conditions as experienced by Sally and Robert. Of course, they have no active memory of their prenatal and formative first two years of life. But they know how good or bad it was from a very early age. What they need is some assistance to organize and make sense of the information they already have.

It is highly inappropriate therefore, to label an individual as an addict. It is for the person to decide with some guidance and assistance.

We can and do talk about behaviours, however, that are indicative of being addicted. It is appropriate to do so insofar as the talk is restricted to factual events. In contrast, to know the soul, where the pot-bellied stove is located, is a matter only the individual can decide.

The Soul and Spirituality

It is difficult to find easy to understand similar definitions for religious concepts. The task is made even more difficult because there is little compelling objective evidence of a soul or in this case a pot-bellied stove that is located there. This reality, however, has not stopped many from discussing at length the soul. Thomas Moore (1992) and others have treated the soul as real and have reflected at length as how best to care for it. If for no other reason than it's utility, accepting the existence of a soul is not such a bad leap in faith. People who do not know that their soul needs to be nourished and consequently do not do so, often find life to be challenging and especially do not do well when life becomes unusually demanding. Life is even more difficult if there is no pot-bellied stove in that soul.

To live a spiritual life is another religious concept difficult to define.

North America's First Nations idea of spirituality offers a good beginning to understanding this critically important concept.

Simply, a spiritual life can be defined as living in harmony with one's self, others and the environment. To live in disharmony therefore, is the cause of much personal, social and environmental problems. For Sally to live like Robert would create critical, if not fatal, disharmony. Because unlike Robert, Sally needs that external source of heat.

In TWO the belief advanced is that the essence of being human is to grow and develop the natural potential with which we are all born. Included in the belief is the need to live in harmony with our environmentally produced life long traits. In this case, for Sally to accept that she has no pot-bellied stove and live accordingly.

If an alligator does not live in harmony with what it is, a cold-blooded creature in need of an external source of heat, it dies. If an addict does not live in harmony with not having an internally generating source of heat, that person also dies, at first figuratively and, in short order, literally. Living a spiritual life for an addict, therefore, requires no more than it does for the alligator. Both need a certain amount of external heat. Depending on conditions sometimes more sometimes less but always some.

Attachment

The literature is quite specific that the greatest trauma perpetrated on an individual is failed attachment. The first relationship for a human is an infant's relationship with, almost always, the mother. The nature of this first relationship sets the tone for all other relationships and how that individual copes or manages the constant challenges life presents from cradle to grave. While there are different types of failed attachment, each involves a primary caregiver, usually the mother, lacking the ability to empathically nurture a child during the formative first two years of life. There are many later-life negative consequences to this, the most significant being repeating dysfunctional family legacies such as the making of addicts. To be sure, if a primary caregiver cannot empathically nurture a child, that mother, father or other caregiver most probably was not empathically nurtured. Sally's story painfully reveals the difficult process that eventually fails in spite of the infant's natural drive to construct that pot-bellied stove and achieve an attachment, if not with mom then with dad.

Most noteworthy about attachment is that when it fails, it is not because of deliberate willful action on the mother's or primary caregiver's part. It is unintended but it is very real. Of equal importance to note is that the ability to empathically nurture can be learned through deliberate, focused effort. There must be motivation, however, to do so, otherwise family histories get repeated and excused by calling on the genetic/inherited explanation.

Splitting

Innately, gestating and new born infants are eager to ingest. They ingest nutrients and they ingest empathic nurturance with which they build the all-important pot-bellied stove and a secure attachment with a primary caregiver.

Given the important role oral ingestion plays in life, it is not surprising that infants can and do experience instinctual oral conflicts. In Sally's case, the need for nutrients both physical and soulful is as innate as is the rejection of it when it is toxic.

This was disturbingly evident in a children's aid case. A child separated from a troubled mother, when reunited for a supervised visit, eagerly ran to her. No sooner did the toddler reach the object of his desire than he started to vomit on her. Without the clinical background information it would have been easy to explain away the incident as indigestion caused by some disagreeable food. This, however, was not the first time the vomiting was observed nor the upset it caused both the mother and the child.

While sometimes true, this symptom of a fundamental disturbance between mother and child, most often is interpreted simply as indigestion caused by certain foods or as indicative of an infant's stomach not having the ability to digest mother's milk.

This interpretation is unfortunate, but to be expected in a climate of abdicating parental, familial and community responsibility for the wellbeing of children. If memory serves, the children's aid worker made a pediatric referral for the toddler, content to interpret the vomiting as indicative of a medical rather than a relational problem.

Admittedly, the existence of a problem had been identified, hence the involvement of the children's aid. However, the conflict between wanting to ingest the good mother and spitting out the toxic elements of her would have provided a much deeper understanding and perhaps a better intervention strategy to help mother and child.

There is no intent here to discount the reality that many children do have colic and can have severe difficulty eating when breast fed. Rather, the intent is to draw attention to the interaction between the mother and her environment; how it impacts on her and in turn, on the child.

Planning

Planning, of which Robert's parents did a great amount, has and continues to have a rather poor reputation. For example, it is said that "what makes God laugh is when people plan", or Robert Burns' famous "The best-laid plans of mice and men often go awry". No doubt they do but how on earth do you achieve anything without a plan? Without a plan, like Sally's family, events just unfold from generation to generation. To change the path, a plan is required. Sally, decided to try that AA program to change how her life was going. This plan is promising for the future, even if it is slightly altered from time to time.

A plan is an observable and measurable goal that is achieved through a number of objectives with the same observable and measurable criteria. It would be a mistake, however, to assume that all the planning in Robert's family turned out as expected. Goals change along with how they are achieved. When that happens there are recalculations in order. Just because plans have to be adjusted does not mean that they are a waste of time. It simply means that life is complex and the basic requirement for adaptability is flexibility and often a revised plan.

Right or Wrong vs The Good

Robert's parents were first taught the difference between doing the wrong and doing the right thing. This is really the only place to start with children until they acquire the ability to think abstractly. Until then, they grasp only the concrete black or white way of evaluating behaviours. Once this foundation is established, they are ready and able to engage with a higher level of reasoning.

The limitations of the right or wrong approach to evaluating or deciding on an action is that at each stage of cognitive development, the right thing to do is differently formulated. For example, for an infant might makes right. Later, the right thing to do is to seize the opportunity and take the path of least resistance to satisfy one's immediate needs, even if it is at the expense of the other. Still later, the right thing to do is that which is valued and prescribed by my reference group or tribe. A reference group can be a religious denomination or an outlaw motorcycle organization. Both are gangs albeit having very different behavioral requirements for membership. For sure they have very different clubhouses.

In a sequence of cognitive development each stage is better than the previous one. At the highest stages, concern for doing the right or wrong thing is replaced by focusing on the good. This translates to doing that which is principled, not an easy to comprehend concept, but one that can be achieved and implemented if prerequisite conditions are satisfied. Robert's parents had the luck of being raised in an environment in which meeting their primary needs (food, shelter, safety, etc.) did not preoccupy them thus freeing them to read, reflect and thereby achieve their natural cognitive developmental potential.

Alas, Sally's parents were consistently under siege, preoccupied with primary needs and escaping the reality of their shit lives. Given this family reality how could they be expected to be aware of, let alone pursue, the good?

The Benefits of Some Steeped in Reality Negativity

The power of positive thinking, an extremely constructive and productive approach to life, has been taken over by those who believe they are required to be positive all the time about everything.

TWO is about first acknowledging that the majority of humanity has been and continues to fail at parenting. As a result, the creation of addicts is globally rampant, along with its many later-life negative consequences. This is not cynicism. This is accepting the existence of a problem and defining what it is. Without this first step, there can be no improvement.

The idea promoted in TWO is markedly different. The position is that humanity has the potential to be noble but is systematically obstructed from becoming it. One obstructing force is those who misinterpret and apply the notion of positive thinking to justify their foolhardy spewing of unwarranted platitudes as to how great or wonderful we are.

When understood and applied as intended, the power of positive thinking can be the motivation to search for ways to unleash the human developmental potential with which we are all born. Robert's story is a good example of what can be achieved and repeated from one generation to the next.

Biological Consequences

Deliberately, the biological consequences of childhood trauma have been understated. There are several reasons for doing so. First, much already has been written about how traumatic stress, neglect and/or abuse impact the developing nervous and endocrine systems of a child. Thus survivors of childhood trauma (eg. failed attachment) are known to have difficulty accessing areas of the brain responsible for higher level adaptive decisions and behaviours. Instead, the responses to challenging situations of such survivors is determined by the limbic and brain stem instinctual systems. Furthermore, since he brain does not complete its development until post adolescence, some contend, that around the age of 25, adverse environmental conditions can and do obstruct this process biologically. These discoveries while critically important have served a dual purpose. The constructive purpose is drawing attention to the importance environment plays in the development of the fetus and the newborn child, specifically during the first two formative years. Less constructive and antithetical to the purpose of writing TWO is that the biological data is used to characterize the making of an addict as an illness or sickness requiring medical treatment.

Second, in contrast to the medical explanation of addiction there is relatively little written about the human soul of addicts let alone the concept of a pot-bellied stove that resides there. Even more importantly, the pot-bellied stove explanation serves the purpose of explaining why the AA twelve step program works, its global prevalence and popularity because of it.

Third, and by no means the least, if TWO is accused of being too simplistic an explanation of a complex phenomenon, especially because the biological consequences have been down played, I say good. An important objective of providing a simple explanation for a complex problem has been achieved. There is far too much reliance on complexity to justify the need for more research and then waiting on the results before we all take responsibility for how we care for the children, almost always, given to us perfect. It is time for an explanation that points to action in which we can all engage rather than looking to a few 'special' people to fix things for us.

A Caution

While necessary, a good pregnancy is not sufficient for ensuring the acquisition of a pot-bellied stove nor a secure attachment of a child to a primary caregiver. A good pregnancy unfortunately can be followed by postpartum depression, marital problems created by the added responsibility of a newborn, the nagging real physical condition colic, and most often lack of knowledge and skills about being a parent, just to name a few possible stressors on one or both parents.

The formative, first two to three years, are just as important, if not more so, than the gestation nine months. Getting prepared for this is absolutely necessary and the best way of doing this is to select and read, both parents, instructional manuals. Newborns don't come with one and hospitals do not send new parents home with one. Fortunately, there are many well written and scientifically proven instructional manuals on the market most commonly known as books on parenting. My personal favourites are by Barbara Cloroso and Thomas Lichona. There are many others and I strongly urge that this type of instructional manual, not like other manuals stored in a drawer but not read, should be read probably many times before and after the baby is born.

Just the Tip of the Iceberg

Not having a pot-bellied stove as a result of being exposed to adverse environmental conditions prenatally and during the most critical first two formative years of life is just the tip of the iceberg. There are many other layers of negative consequences, each requiring its own systematic examination. At least listing the most debilitating ones should serve to underscore two important points, which are the broad objectives of writing TWO. The first is to convey how important those 33 months are and how conditions shape who we become. The second is to convey that it is far easier and cost effective to devise and implement a long-term preventative strategy. Most current reactive efforts are comparatively futile, notwithstanding that indeed addicted addicts can get and stay sober as long as they attend AA. Once sober, the other required work can begin. For example, when sober many learn about their demons and use the knowledge to control them. But it is a life-long task that requires constant vigilance since there is no cure for being an addict.

Adverse environment conditions during the early years almost always include a real threat to the very life of the infant. This is experienced instinctively and stored in the limbic system as critically important information for survival. Because of the importance of the information, the interpretation of external stimuli is not mediated by the *rational* parts of the brain. Consequently, the most common feelings triggered by external stimuli for people like Sally are fear or sadness. Cognitively, she is predisposed to distort any and all events to be severe and to react accordingly. In fear, she considers her very life to be threatened and reacts in an aggressive, defensive manner. It's a reaction often mistakenly considered to be a problem with "anger management".

Most of the violent offenders, I've encountered, regardless of the focus of their violence, are in a constant emotional state of fear. This includes those who commit domestic violence.

Similarly, people like Sally, when not operating from the emotional state of fear, are almost always sad. The sadness gives them more reason to seek escape through some mood-altering behaviour, most often involving the ingestion of some drug.

Obstructed cognitive developmental potential is yet another devastating consequence of adverse early-life experiences. Regardless of average or better cognitive intelligence chronologically advanced but developmentally obstructed individuals like Sally behave like impetuous hedonistic children who are always seeking immediate gratification of needs. They are given various labels, the most familiar category being personality disorders. Not having learned to regulate their emotions and to curtail their impulses, they behave badly and wreak havoc for themselves and anyone in their path. They don't suffer from a medical condition. They simply never had the chance to develop their cognitive potential, grow up and, as a result, behave badly in readily recognizable narcissistic, histrionic or antisocial ways.

To reiterate, the effort and often the futility of putting out the later-life negative consequence fires caused by adverse early life experiences is all too familiar. Nevertheless, dealing with the symptoms is far more palatable than admitting to the underlying problem. That the addict who almost always becomes addicted and behaves badly in a variety of different ways is of our own creation. Admit to it, however, we must if sustainable change is ever going to be achieved.

IF YOU DISAGREE WITH THIS STORY OF TWO FAMILIES, ONE MAKING AN ADDICT THE OTHER NOT, WHAT IS YOUR EXPLANATION AND SOLUTION FOR THIS PERVASIVE INSIDIOUS HUMAN PROBLEM?

ACKNOWLEDGEMENTS

I am eternally grateful to Drina, the love of my life, for letting me, tolerating me and encouraging me to continue my lifelong pursuit of tilting at windmills. Without her quiet but palpable support my quixotian quest would be lonely and probably intolerable. Probably I would have given up long ago trying to make life better than I found it.

I am grateful to have known many addicted addicts who trustfully shared their personal stories from which I learned and developed the formulations on which TWO is based. They have been some of the best teachers I have ever encountered.

I am equally grateful for the myriad of events and types of people I have encountered that have stirred my constantly unsatisfied quest for understanding and from this scheming to make things better. I am even grateful for having the audacity to think that I can be, in a small way, instrumental in improving our understanding of what it means to be an addicted addict and doing something about it.

I am also grateful for my early life experiences which allowed me to quickly, without lingering too long, pass through the unavoidable tribal reference group stage perspective. This has freed me from being preoccupied with peer approval and especially from striving to become part of the establishment. Being on the outside has made it easier to avoid becoming an inadvertent status quo maintainer especially of ideas not particularly useful for solving certain problems.

I am especially grateful for having Karen Rachner in my professional life. Without her patient toil, enduring several revisions and edits, this and other works of mine would have not been possible.

I am also extremely grateful for the sage counsel, advice and guidance of Grant D. Fairley. Without him TWO seeing the light of day would have taken at least twice as long.

Last but not least I am grateful for the few but significant like-minded individuals who dare to speak the truth to power, who dare to challenge the establishment, who think outside of the proverbial box. Without knowing, they have inspired my thinking and gave me the courage to expose my ideas in the written word for all to see.

ABOUT THE AUTHOR

Alexander T. Polgar Ph.D. is a persistent and ever curious learner. He has combined in a forty-eight year span several parallel careers grounded in a passionate pursuit to improve the individual and the collective human condition. TWO, which is the first book in the trilogy about addicts, who invariably become addicted, is the product of his accumulative experience assessing and treating individuals traumatized during gestation and the critically important formative years of life. Born out of satisfied curiosity he has long ago abandoned the medical model establishment explanation of most bad behaviour especially that of addicts. Instead, he has dared to pursue understanding, through reason and science, the tenets of enlightenment, where addicts come from and what it means to be one.

REFERENCES

Aron, E.N. (1996). **The highly sensitive person: How to thrive when the world overwhelms you.** New York: Harmony Books.

Coloroso, Barbara (1994). **Kids are worth it.** Toronto: Summerville House Publishing.

Condrad, P., and Schneider, J.W. (1992). **Deviance and medicalization: From badness to sickness.** Philadelphia: Temple University Press.

Duncan, B.L., and Miller, S.D. (2000). **The heroic client.** San Francisco: Jossey Bass Inc..

Komer, L.D., and Komer, J.L. (2016). **New hope for concussions, TBI & PTSD.** Toronto: Peak Performance Publishing.

Lickona, Thomas (1994). **Raising good children: From birth through the teenage years.** New York: Bantam Books.

Maté, G. (2008). **In the realm of hungry ghosts: Close encounter with addiction.** Canada: Alfred A. Knopf.

Moncrieff, J. (2009). **The myth of the chemical cure: A critique of psychiatric drug treatment.** New York: Palgrave Macmillan.

Moore, Thomas (1994). **Care of the soul.** New York, N.Y.: Harper Collins Publishers.

Polgar, A.T. (2009). **Because we can – we must: Achieving the human developmental potential.** Hamilton, Ontario: Sandriam Publications.

Read, J., Mosher, L.R., and Bental, R.P. (2004). **Models of madness.** London: Routledge.

SANDRIAM

PUBLICATIONS